I0815358

SNEAKERHEADS

CONVERSE

KENNY ABDO

Fly!
An Imprint of Abdo Zoom
abdobooks.com

abdobooks.com

Published by Abdo Zoom, a division of ABDO, P.O. Box 398166, Minneapolis, Minnesota 55439.

Printed in the United States of America, North Mankato, Minnesota.
102024
012025

Photo Credits: Alamy, AP Images, Depositphotos Enterprise, Getty Images, Shutterstock, ©TyeTheDye75 p12 / CC BY-SA
Production Contributors: Kenny Abdo, Jennie Forsberg, Grace Hansen
Design Contributors: Candice Keimig, Neil Klinepier, Laura Graphenteen

Library of Congress Control Number: 2024936561

Publisher's Cataloging-in-Publication Data

Names: Abdo, Kenny, author.
Title: Converse / by Kenny Abdo
Description: Minneapolis, Minnesota : Abdo Zoom, 2025 | Series: Sneakerheads | Includes online resources and index.
Identifiers: ISBN 9781098287450 (lib. bdg.) | ISBN 9781098288150 (ebook) | ISBN 9781098288501 (Read-to-me ebook)
Subjects: LCSH: Sneakers--Juvenile literature. | Shoes--Juvenile literature. | Fashion--Social aspects--Juvenile literature. | Converse (Firm)--Juvenile literature.
Classification: DDC 391.413--dc23

TABLE OF CONTENTS

Converse.......................... 4

The OGs 8

The Kicks 12

The Restock...................... 26

Glossary 30

Online Resources 31

Index 32

CONVERSE

Made with just a little bit of fabric and rubber, no one imagined that Converse shoes would become one of the most **iconic** sneakers ever!

CONVERSE
ALL STAR
Chuck
70

NBA

Converse has its footprints all over basketball, the **Olympics**, and pop culture. The shoes have made a mark on history!

THE OGs

Marquis Mills Converse started the Converse Rubber Shoe Company in Massachusetts in 1908. The business made footwear and items such as car tires. Around the same time, a game-changing sport was becoming popular close by.

C

Professional basketball was sweeping the East Coast. In 1915, Converse **debuted** the Non-Skid shoe for the sport. In 1919, it was renamed the All Star.

THE KICKS

Charles Taylor began working at Converse in 1922. He was also a semi-professional basketball player. Taylor offered suggestions to make the shoe better for the sport. It was re-released in 1923 with a new name: the Chuck Taylor All Star.

Taylor hit the road to promote the All Star. The American **Olympic** Basketball team wore the shoe for the 1936 games! The shoe's popularity soared. Even US soldiers wore All Stars while training for **World War II**.

COMPANIES F & G
CLASS II
BEGINNER TRAINEES -
DISABILITIES
KNEE-QUADRICEPS

The low top All Star **debuted** in 1957, making the **brand** popular on and off the court. Stars such as James Dean and Elvis Presley sported the classic high tops!

CONVERSE
ALL
CONVERSE
ALL

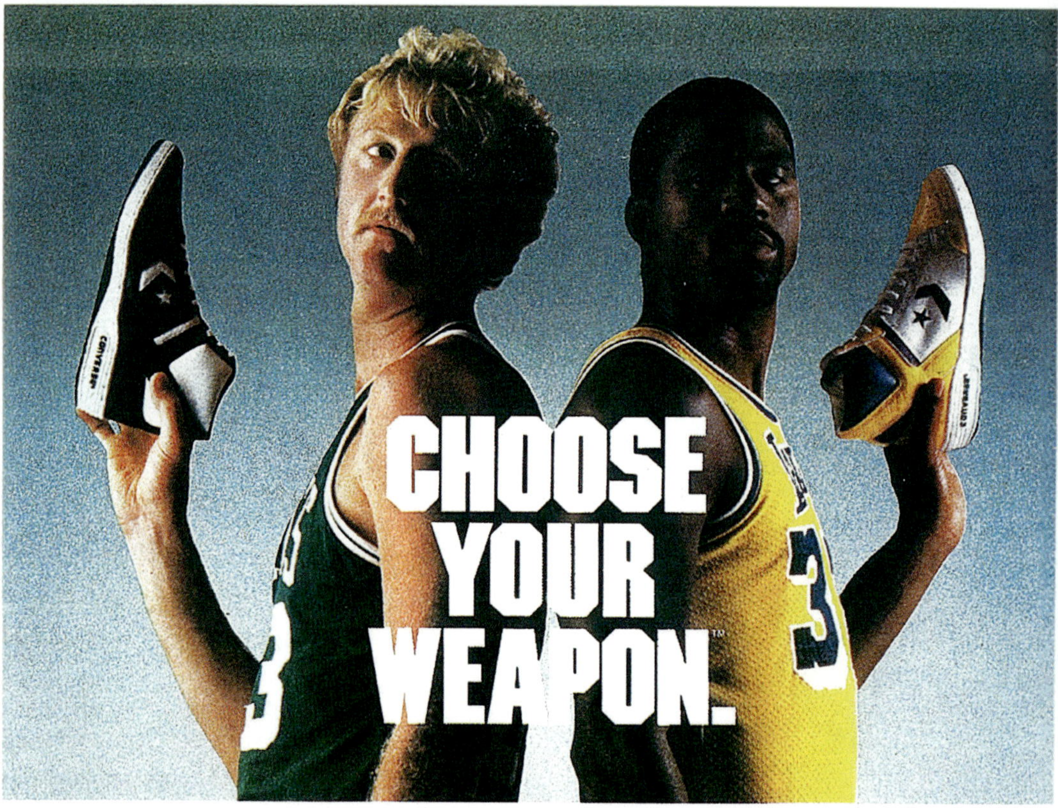

CHOOSE YOUR WEAPON.™

Larry Bird and Magic Johnson. When they play, they push themselves to the limit. And they trust their performance to Converse. The shoe they choose to do battle in is the Converse® Weapon™– a shoe biomechanically designed to help players play their best.

These shoes offer superior traction because of their natural rubber outsoles. They're incredibly cushioned as well, due to the Center of Pressure outsole and a shock absorbing EVA midsole. And for the strong ankle support that Bird, Magic and every other ballplayer needs, there's the unique Y-Bar Ankle Support System.

Besides all these features, the Converse Weapon has a comfortable, removable insole and an extra padded collar that combines with the Y-Bar System for enhanced ankle support and comfort.

Bird and Magic have chosen their weapons. Now choose yours.

The Converse Weapon. One more reason why athletes like Bird and Magic depend on Converse for the best possible performance.

The Pro Leather basketball sneaker **debuted** in the '70s. The shoe was worn by NBA greats such as Larry Bird and Magic Johnson. Meanwhile, bands like Led Zeppelin and The Ramones continued to rock the **OGs**.

All Stars steadily became staples of hip hop and rock fashion. Artists like Kurt Cobain, Snoop Dogg, and The Rolling Stones put the star in All Star!

VMA

CONVERSE
ALL STAR

To everyone's surprise, Converse filed for **bankruptcy** in 2001. Nike bought the company in 2003. By 2013, Nike had taken the **brand** from ruin to must-have!

Converse has had many successful **collaborations** by working with **iconic** fashion **brands** like KITH, Off-White, and Carhartt. This has kept the shoes on sneakerheads' radars!

"VULCANIZED"

THE RESTOCK

Some All Star fans wanted a piece of history. In 2017, Michael Jordan's game-worn Converse shoes were **auctioned** off.

They went for more than $190,000 to become the most expensive pair of Converse in the world!

Converse has seen a lot of change in its time. Yet, the All Stars have kept the same design since 1949. This proves that no one should mess with perfection!

CONVERSE
Chuck Taylor
ALL STAR

GLOSSARY

auction – a sale at which goods are sold to the highest bidder.

bankrupt – legally lacking funds needed to pay off money owed.

brand – a name, design, or symbol that separates one product from another.

collaboration – to work with another person or group to do something or reach a goal.

debut – a first appearance.

iconic – widely known or easily recognized.

OG – someone or something that is an original or creator. Usually highly respected.

Olympic Games – the biggest sporting event in the world that is divided into summer and winter games.

World War II – (1939–1945) a war fought in Europe, Asia, and Africa. Great Britain, France, the United States, the Soviet Union, and their allies were on one side. Germany, Italy, Japan, and their allies were on the other side.

ONLINE RESOURCES

To learn more about Converse, please visit **abdobooklinks.com** or scan this QR code. These links are routinely monitored and updated to provide the most current information available.

INDEX

All-Star (shoe) 11, 13, 16, 19, 20, 26, 28
Bird, Larry 19
Carhartt (brand) 24
Cobain, Kurt 20
Converse Rubber Company 9
Converse, Marquis Mills 9
Dogg, Snoop 20
Johnson, Magic 19
Jordan, Michael 26
KITH (brand) 24
Led Zeppelin (band) 19
low tops (shoe) 16
Nike (brand) 23
Off-White (brand) 24
Olympics 7, 14
Pro Leather (shoe) 19
Ramones, The (band) 19
Rolling Stones, The (band) 20
Taylor, Charles 13, 14
World War II 14